INTO THE THICK OF IT

WORDS THOUGHT BUT NEVER SAID

G.A. Files

Into The Thick of It

Words Thought But Never Said

© 2021 G.A. Files

Presentation by BookLeaf Publishing

Web: www.bookleafpub.com

E-mail: info@bookleafpub.com

ISBN : 9789358362138

First edition 2021

To everyone who dreams, and everyone
who is different.

1

Let me tell you something straight off.

Writers don't write for fun.

They write so that their mind doesn't explode,

Ideas pouring from their fingers faster than they can write. Faster than they can think.

They write so they can sleep without worlds and words dancing behind their eyelids.

It's dreaming while awake, vivid imaginings of places no one has ever seen and people no one has ever met.

Only writers and crazy people hear voices in their heads.

And those two groups are not mutually exclusive.

They create life, breathing it into characters relatable and comforting. Surprising and disturbing.

Equally human.

They write to deal with emotions, with their frustrations, their highs and lows,

Giving voice to things others might not know how to express but feel--oh they feel!--so strongly.

The cozy feeling of a warm blanket on a rainy day, droplets sliding down window panes, and a drink steaming beside you.

The despair of love unrequited, love denied, love lost.

The joy and sorrow that comes from the human experience.

Writers write to distance themselves.

Writers write to connect.

Writers don't write for fun.

They write because they have to.

2

Poetry is like yoga for the brain,

Stretching your mind past its limits, past its comfort zone.

Utilizing space.

Utilizing silence.

3

Present me and future me are usually at odds, though they do often agree that neither of them like past me very much.

(It's the procrastination.)

Although present me is past me to my future self, so maybe it's just past me everyone has beef with.

Or tofurky if you're vegetarian.

4

I carry my failures in my stomach, my ass,
my breasts, my thighs.

My failure to exercise more than I eat,

To always eat healthily as well as happily.

My failure to moderate, to meditate,

To migrate somewhere other than from the
bed to the couch.

I hold my failure to impress,

My failure to dress with style and pizazz,

To work for the body I want rather than eat
what I want.

The biggest failure though, is the one in my
heart.

The failure to love who I am, what I look
like,

To be proud of what my body can do, what it has accomplished.

This failure in being unable to look beyond other people's ideas of what beauty looks like, what beauty is.

It is more harmful, more toxic, more prevalent than just my individual shortcomings.

It is a failure of my world.

It is a failure I will not carry forward, or pass on.

Failing is just a lesson in what has not worked. Yet.

5

A friendly reminder that you are only you
to you.

A different version of you exists in the
minds of everyone you've ever known.

It's not that to your parents you're a child,
or to your brother or sister you're a sibling.

To your father, you're the miracle doctors
told him he could never have.

You are your mother's legacy.

Your grandmother's revenge.

You are victim and villain,

Vilified and vindicated.

A playmate, a helpmate, a soulmate.

You are a source of envy, and wonder, pity
and disdain.

You are a comfort, a guilty pleasure, a
confidant, a safe place.

You are a flake, a steady hand, a shoulder to
cry on.

You are a trustworthy friend.

You are somebody's foe.

A different version of you exists in the
minds of everyone you know.

6

There's a lump in my breast.

I want to tell everyone.

I want to tell no one.

There's an ache in my chest.

It's not only from my heart, but the
discoloured skin I can see in the mirror.

What diagnosis is best?

A possible infection?

The big C? (Not Corona this time. The
original big C).

I just need some rest.

The exhaustion, uncertainty, the pain,

The desire to scream out with the what ifs
and what nows?

There's a lump in my breast.

I want to die.

I want to live.

7

I can feel it. It's a physical ache.

A throbbing in my chest that I'm aware of.

Unnatural.

Sick.

Something's wrong.

And all I can do is wait.

Wait for doctors, wait for tests,

Wait to get off shift so I can try to find
answers. (Work to live, live to work!)

Because I can feel it.

It's a physical ache.

Growing under my skin,

Hardening my breast like armour.

Except it won't protect me. It'll kill me.

8

They told us we'd be safe.

We said never again.

They lied.

We said never again.

It turns out the memory of the world is just
shy of 80 years.

We said never again.

They always need a scape goat.

We said never again.

They tell us to get out.

We said never again.

Get out before they come for you.

We said never again.

And they will come for you.

We said never again.

There is only one place we will be safe.
Welcomed with open arms.

We said never again.

And they want to burn that too.

We said never again.

Drive us into the sea.

We said never again.

We said never again.

9

The part that upsets me the most about
potentially dying prematurely

is leaving my cats alone.

Even now, they wait at the door to my
bedroom

(I don't let them sleep with me).

Do they understand when I've gone out that
I've actually gone?

Or do they think I'm still on the other side
of the door, but ignoring them?

Is that what death is?

The part that upsets me the most about
potentially dying prematurely

is leaving my cats alone.

The thought that they won't understand.

That they'll think I've abandoned them like everyone else in their young lives.

One was surrendered twice prior to my getting her.

I promised her I'd be her forever home.

I promised them both.

The part that upsets me the most about potentially dying prematurely

is leaving my cats alone.

They drive me crazy--so crazy!

But I love them.

They love me.

If I go before them, they won't understand, will they?

They'll just think one day I never came home.

Never came back for them.

What a strange thing to be worried about, a cat's concept of death.

10

I don't just have a love-hate relationship
with my body.

I have a love-love

Hate-hate.

I love my body.

Hate when I hate it.

Hate that I love it, and don't improve it,

Love that I hate myself into working out.

Love when I love it, and love when I hate
people who hate it.

People say it's mind over matter, but matter
and mind have to coexist.

And that's a whole other story.

11

You don't exist for yourself.

You're a woman, how could you?

You are here to make your parents proud,

To set an example for your siblings.

You are here for men to sexualize and objectify.

To provide them with desires, and to accept the consequences of those same desires.

The blame.

The shame.

You are here to be a mother.

Your body is not your own.

It belongs to everyone else.

It's meant to nurture and sustain, but not you. Never you.

12

Be successful but not proud.

Be pretty but not beautiful.

Be smart but not nerdy.

Be gentle but not a wimp.

Be kind but not a doormat.

Take care of yourself but don't be selfish.

Take care of others but don't nag.

Take opportunities but don't take advantage.

Don't do everything yourself, but don't ask for help.

Don't be a working mother, but don't just stay at home either.

Be what everyone else wants you to be, but why can't you ever just be yourself?

13

Safety.

You don't know the meaning of the word until you're halfway across the world watching bombs light up the sky in your second home.

In your head you can hear the sirens.

In your heart you can feel the fear.

But there's no danger to you.

There are no rockets falling.

Your sleep is interrupted by worry, not the very real potential of being killed by a bomb.

You could sleep if your mind would let you.

You are not forced to flee to a bomb shelter every half hour, terrified that this run might be your last.

Hoping it will be.

You don't have to lie on the floor of a motionless bus, waiting. Hoping. Praying.

Or go careening headlong into a ditch with strangers,

Hoping this will be protection enough.

Worse still to have no protection at all.

To know that your government wants you to die.

There is more value in your death.

They place you in harm's way hoping that harm will find you,

Knowing that when it does, they will not even be blamed.

It will in fact serve their purpose. Their narrative.

Can you imagine?

You can't. And that is safety. That is privilege.

14

The sirens blare overhead.

The map of the country is covered with red.

They want the streets to run the same shade.

They get more money for every corpse that is made.

Israeli, Palestinian, they don't give a damn.

Every death serves a purpose, child, woman, or man.

Politicians, terrorists, playing with people's lives.

Children are taught to go after others with knives.

With stones in their hands and stones in their hearts,

Every action intended to drive us further apart.

15

Women these days get to have it all.

As if it's some great privilege to never drop the ball.

Running on no sleep, always at a frenetic pace,

Trying to be everything to everyone, to put on a brave face.

Mother, daughter, sister, wife,

If we're not each of these things, what is the point of life?

There is no simple ""just enough,"" women must excel.

Any failure on our parts sets others back as well.

And don't think we can ask for help; that's admitting defeat.

Not being able to manage, expectations we cannot meet.

Choose to be only one, and you're missing out.

Try to be everything to everyone, that's what it's all about.

They say women get to do everything,

But they have to, not get to, and it's just tiring.

16

There's a boy in my bed.

A boy--a man--a boy.

With stubbled cheeks, but a smile as he dreams.

He looks younger like this.

Clean skin against clean sheets.

Cradled in my bed.

In my arms.

Like a babe, he reaches for me in his sleep.

Without waking, he latches on, pulling me closer.

He tugs on my heart as surely as he tugs on my limbs.

We say, ""Be a man! Act like a man!""

But why can't men stay boys with their cheeky smiles, and looks of wonder?

17

There's a girl in my bed.

This girl still has her dreams, safely stored
in her pillow, her innocence protected by
her sheets.

Her mattress cradles her, holds her,
supports her.

She comes here for soothing, for rest.

Eyes can safely close, tears shed.

Worries released.

Fears whispered to a teddy bear's
unjudgemental ears.

There's a girl in my bed with an undimmed
smile,

Undiminished hopes.

She still believes she can do anything,

Say anything.

Be anything.

And so do I.

18

28

Disdain,

Deny,

Refrain,

Decry.

Silence in the face of pain,

Or mayhap you let out a sigh.

You once swore never again

And yet now you let them die.

Disdain,

Deny,

Refrain,

Decry.

Though your hands might not have slain,

Your inaction shows the lie

In the words spoken in vain

Meant only to pacify.

Disdain,

Deny,

Refrain,

Decry.

When sympathy you only feign,

And empty morality you supply,

On your hands will lie the stain

Of the harm done whilst you turned a blind
eye.

Disdain,

Deny,

Refrain,

Decry.

Of one thing you must make certain,

Stand up and say fie!

To others you must explain

The dangers of silence; don't let the opportunity pass you by.

19

Have you ever noticed that the image you see with your eyes, and through a camera is never the same?

You cannot capture a picture of the moon that you see before you, big, bright and brilliant.

Or the colours of the sunset.

Or the star filled vastness of the night sky.

You can only experience it.

Bask in it.

Feel the wonder in the face of all that beauty and majesty.

Did you ever think that you might be the same way?

Your beauty cannot be expressed in a reflection, a camera lens.

You too are a natural wonder, unable to be contained in a single image.

20

There is poetry everywhere you look,

Music all around.

In the pages of the book

In the thrumming of the ground.

Not just the birds in the trees,

Though they do sing sweetly.

But listen to the buzzing of the bees,

Who pollinate so neatly.

Take note too of the water, babbling in the
creek,

And the lapping of the waves gentle upon
the sand.

They carry the answers that you seek,

But do not reveal them on command.

9 789358 362138